# MY PRETTY PINK

# Sticker
## Purse

Pull out the sticker sheets and keep them
by you when you complete each page.
There are also lots of extra stickers to
use in this book or anywhere you want!

make
believe
ideas

# Garden pals

Use color and stickers to complete the scene.

Decorate Pinky the unicorn with pretty pink hearts.

How many toadstools can you count? Sticker the answer.

# Tasty treats

Use stickers to
complete the patterns.

# Bunny's burrows

Help Betty Bunny find her friend and then sticker the missing carrots.

How many carrots can you count? Sticker the answer.

Sticker the missing carrots.

# Accessorize!

Use stickers to give Emma
lots of pretty pink accessories.

Color the nail polish
in pretty shades.

# Sherbet Forest

Princess Poppy is lost in Sherbet Forest!
Sticker a trail of marshmallows
to lead her to the castle.

Sticker birds
in the nests.

Give each squirrel
an acorn to eat.

How many pink flowers can you count? Sticker the answer.

Color the cute fawn!

# A trip to Pink Park

Pink Park is busy today!
Read and trace the words below,
then find the missing stickers.

dog

duck

flower

tree

# Toadstool Town

Use stickers and color to help
the fairies turn the toadstools
into pretty homes.

# Farmyard fun

Use stickers to help
Farmer Fred finish the sums.

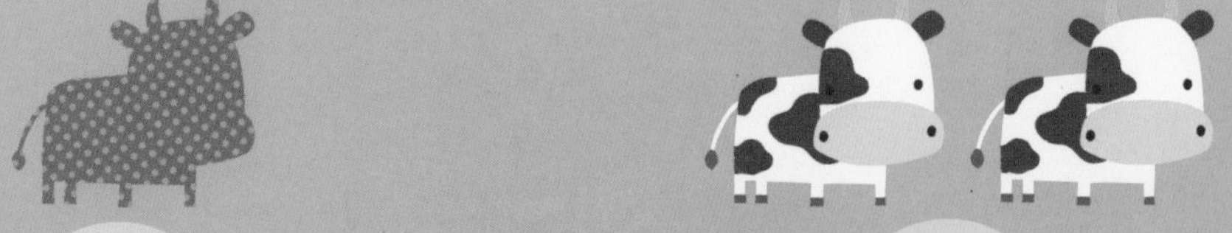

1 + 2 =

2 + 2 =

2 + 3 =

Color the
tractor pink.

# Bake a cake!

Find the missing stickers
to help Carrie bake a cake!

MILK

Trace the spiral
to mix the batter.

Use stickers and color to help Carrie decorate the cake.

# Bubble trouble!

Use stickers to match the bubble shapes to the correct labels.

star

heart

boat

fish

Color the bubbles pink!

# Wiggly pigs!

The pigs are creating a wiggly tower
to reach the treats in the tree.

Sticker the
missing pigs.

How many pigs
can you count?
Sticker the answer.

# Cute creatures

Sticker and doodle to change the shapes into pretty pink pictures.

# Time for tea

The toys are having a tea party! Sticker the missing toys and teacups.

How many crowns can you count? Sticker the answer.

Sticker cupcakes on the plates.

# Rainbow Road

Mailman Mike is delivering post.
Sticker the correct colored
letter for each person.

Gregory Green

Pippa Pink

# Pretty patterns

Use stickers to complete the pretty patterns.

# Flower garden

Use color and stickers to make a
beautiful garden, full of butterflies and bees.

How many butterflies
can you count?
Sticker the answer.

# Yo-ho-ho!

The pink pirates are setting out on a voyage.
Use color and stickers to finish their ship.

Design a pink pirate flag.

How many mice can you count? Sticker the answer.

Sticker the missing jewels, and circle the one that doesn't match.

# Lovely lunch

Follow the trails to match
each animal to its lunch.

# All aboard!

Can you spot five differences between the two trains?

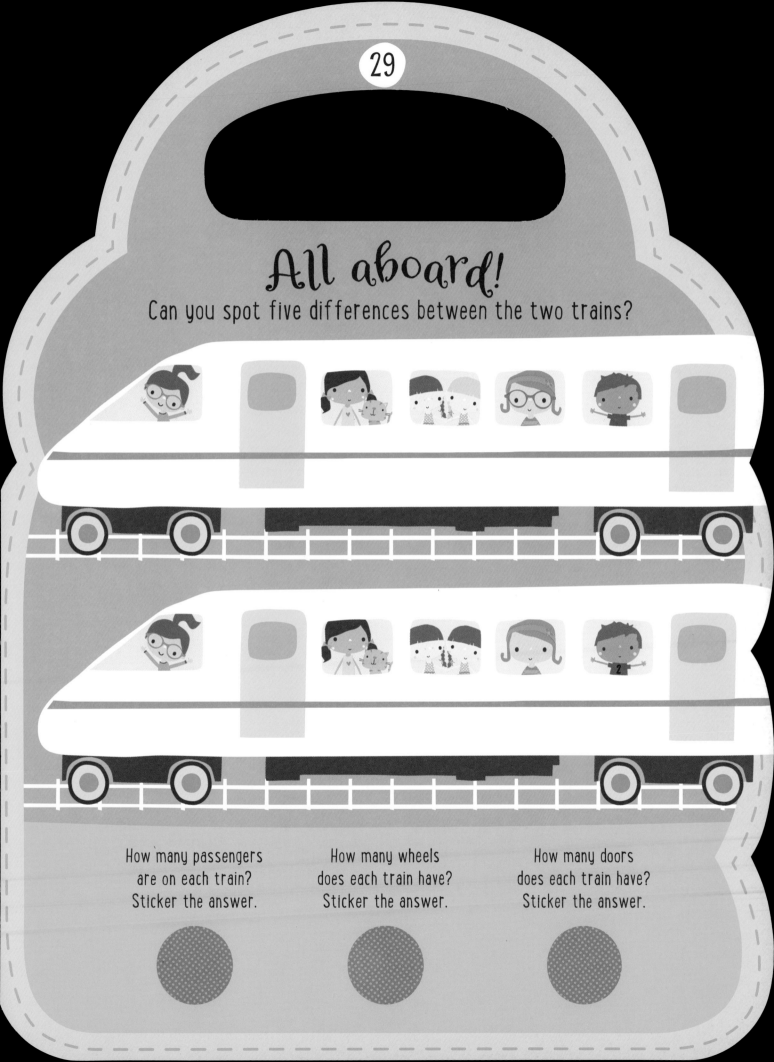

How many passengers are on each train? Sticker the answer.

How many wheels does each train have? Sticker the answer.

How many doors does each train have? Sticker the answer.

# Monster munchers

The mini monsters are making an enormous sandwich.

Draw the fillings you would have in your perfect sandwich.

Circle five beetles hiding in the food.

Give the blue monsters forks.

Sticker more fillings in the sandwich.

# Pink Planet

Trace the dots to create
pretty pictures in the stars.

Sticker more
stars in the sky.

Color the brave
space explorers.

# Cats in hats

Sticker a stylish hat on each cat.

Color this cat's cute sun hat.

# Pink panic!

Something has turned
the laundry pink!

Color the
clothes pink.

Can you find the red sock in the machine?

Sticker the
missing clothes.

# Animal pairs

Find the missing stickers, then draw
a line to match the moms and babies.

# Cute collections

Find the missing stickers to help Prince Peter and Princess Pippa finish their collections. Then circle the one that doesn't match in each collection.

One of these is not pink.

One of these is not a fruit.

One of these is not an animal.

# Beautiful balloons

Decorate the pretty hot-air balloons with color and stickers.

Look at the picture and check the boxes when you find the things in the list.

1 barn

2 horses

3 cows

1 tractor

# Under the sea

Use color and stickers to complete the underwater scene. Can you find ten pink sea horses?

# Pretty princess ball

The princesses are getting ready for the ball. Use color and stickers to give them beautiful outfits.

# Pretty pink quiz

Find the missing stickers, then circle the correct answer to each question.

Can you find the sleeping cat?

Which animal lays eggs?

hen

hamster

rhinoceros

Who goes cheep-cheep?

koala

chick

rabbit

spider

snake

Which animal has a shell?

frog

fox

squirrel

parrot

tortoise

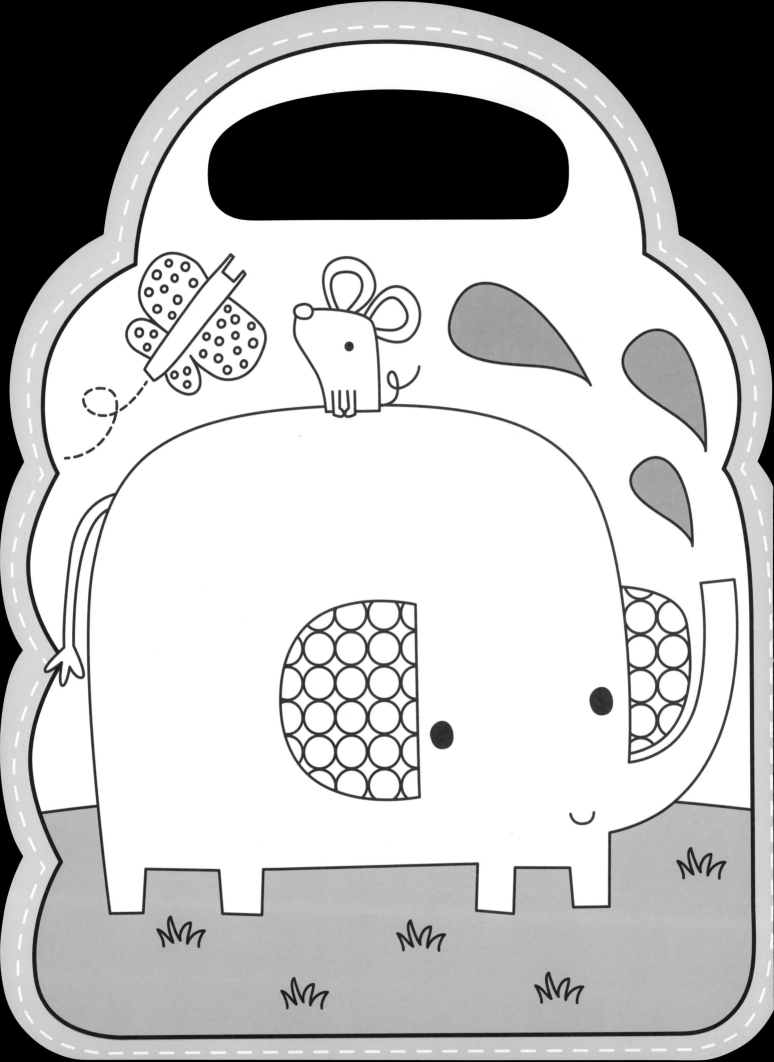

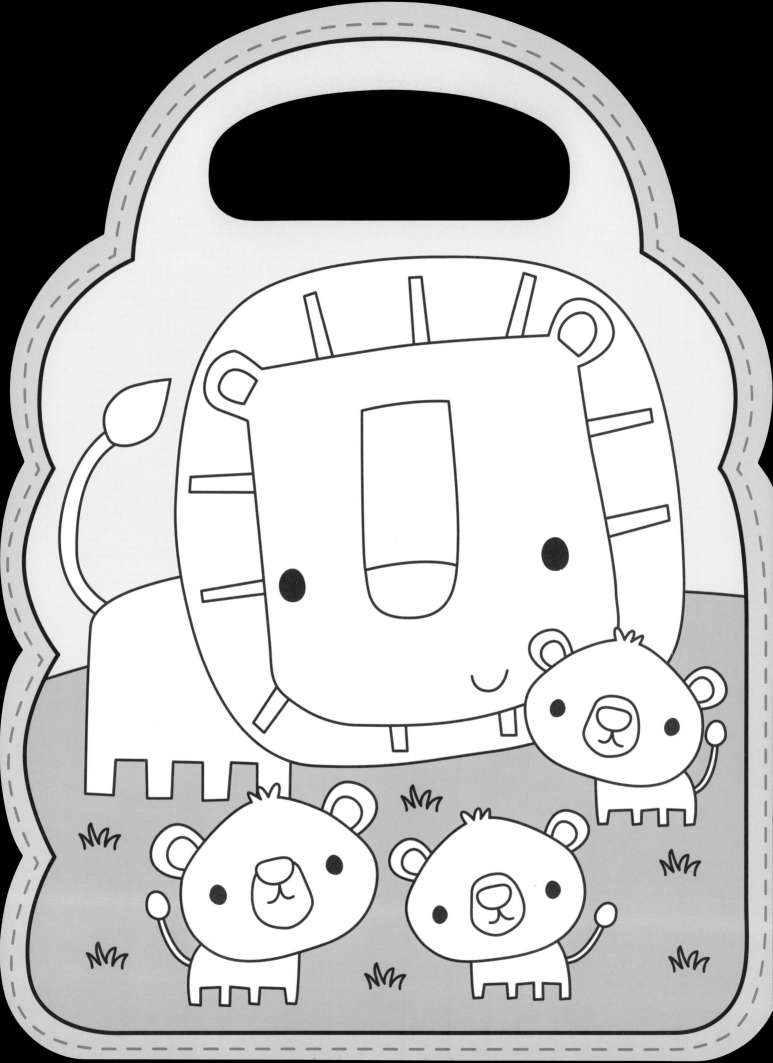

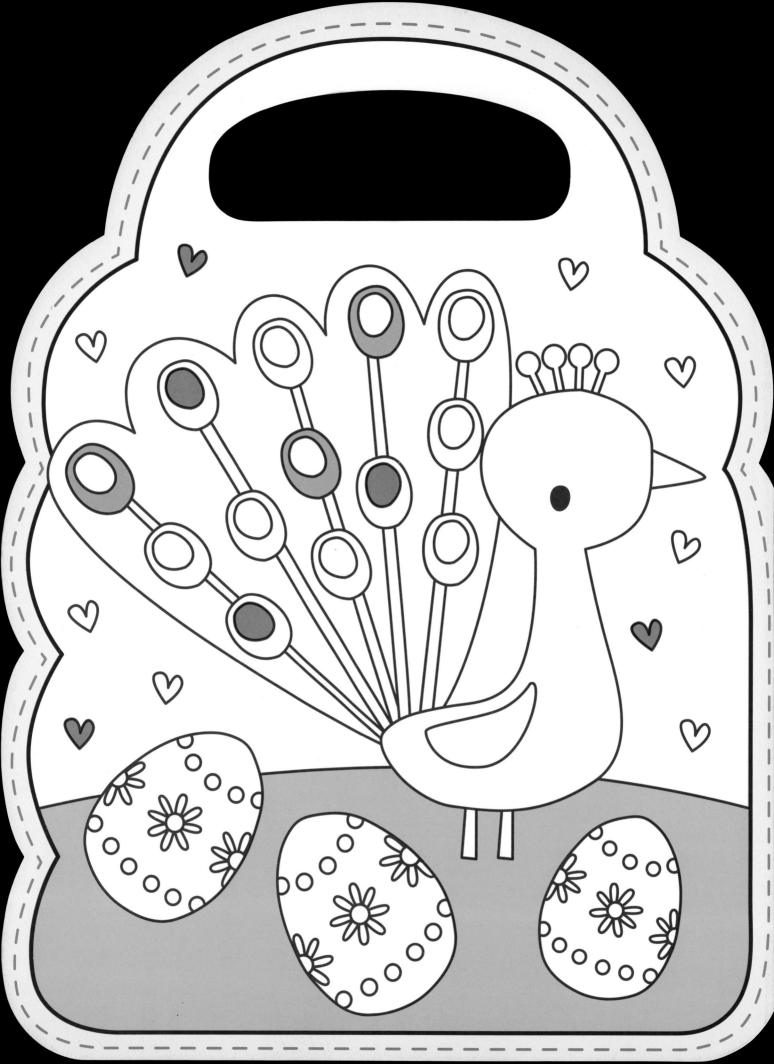